Copyright © 2015 Sci Fi Coloring

All Rights Reserved Worldwide

SCI FI
Coloring Book

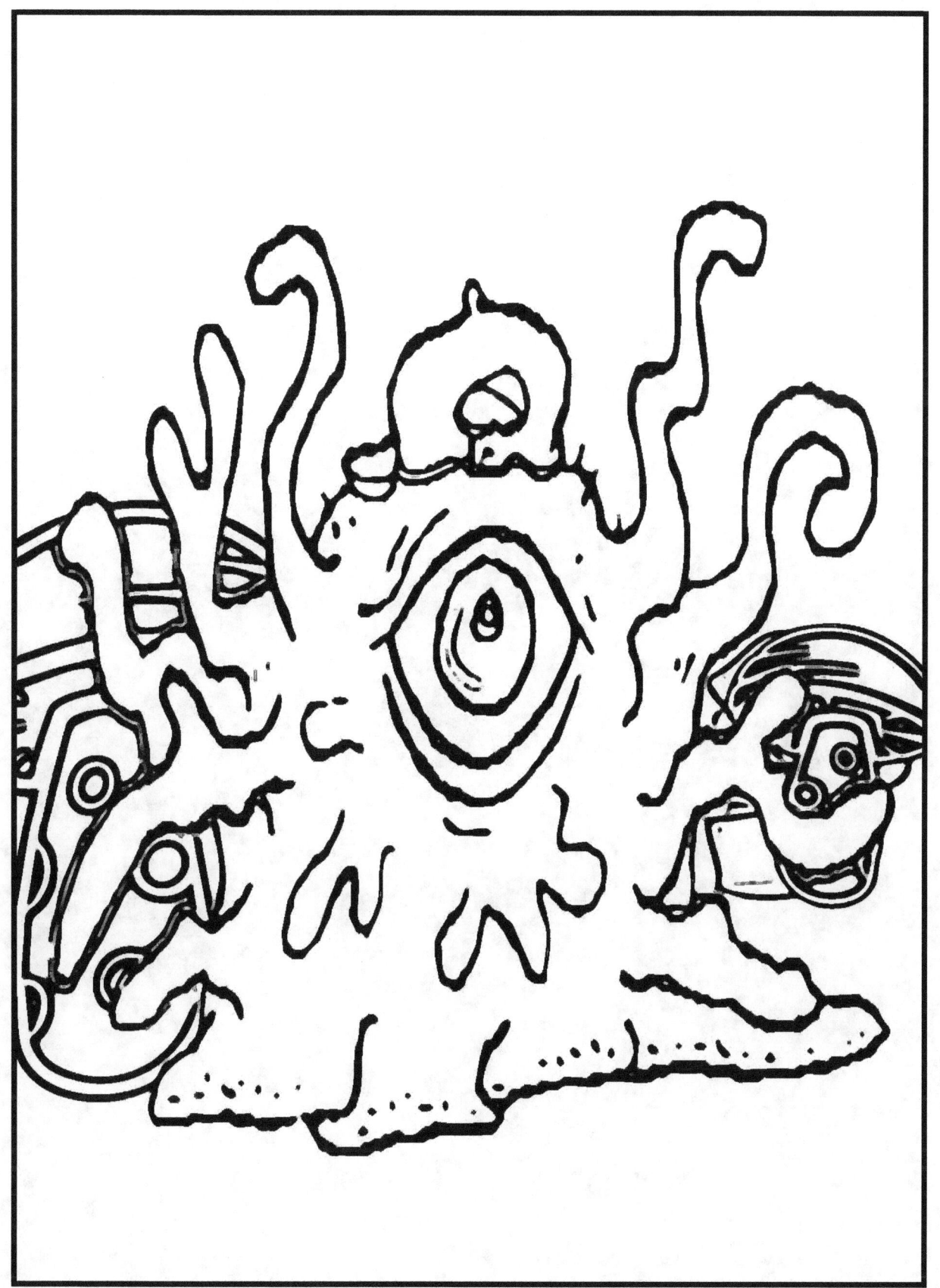

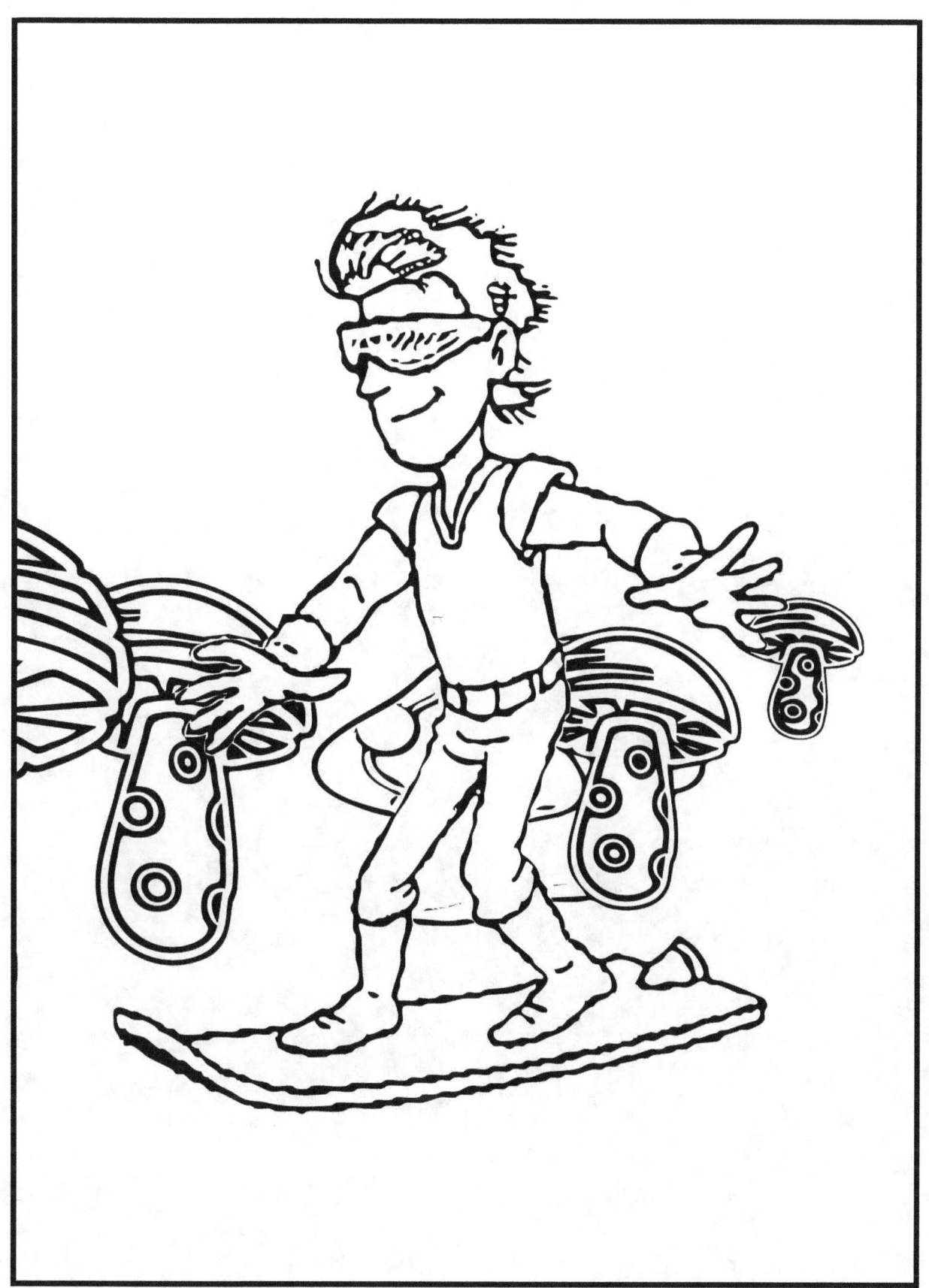

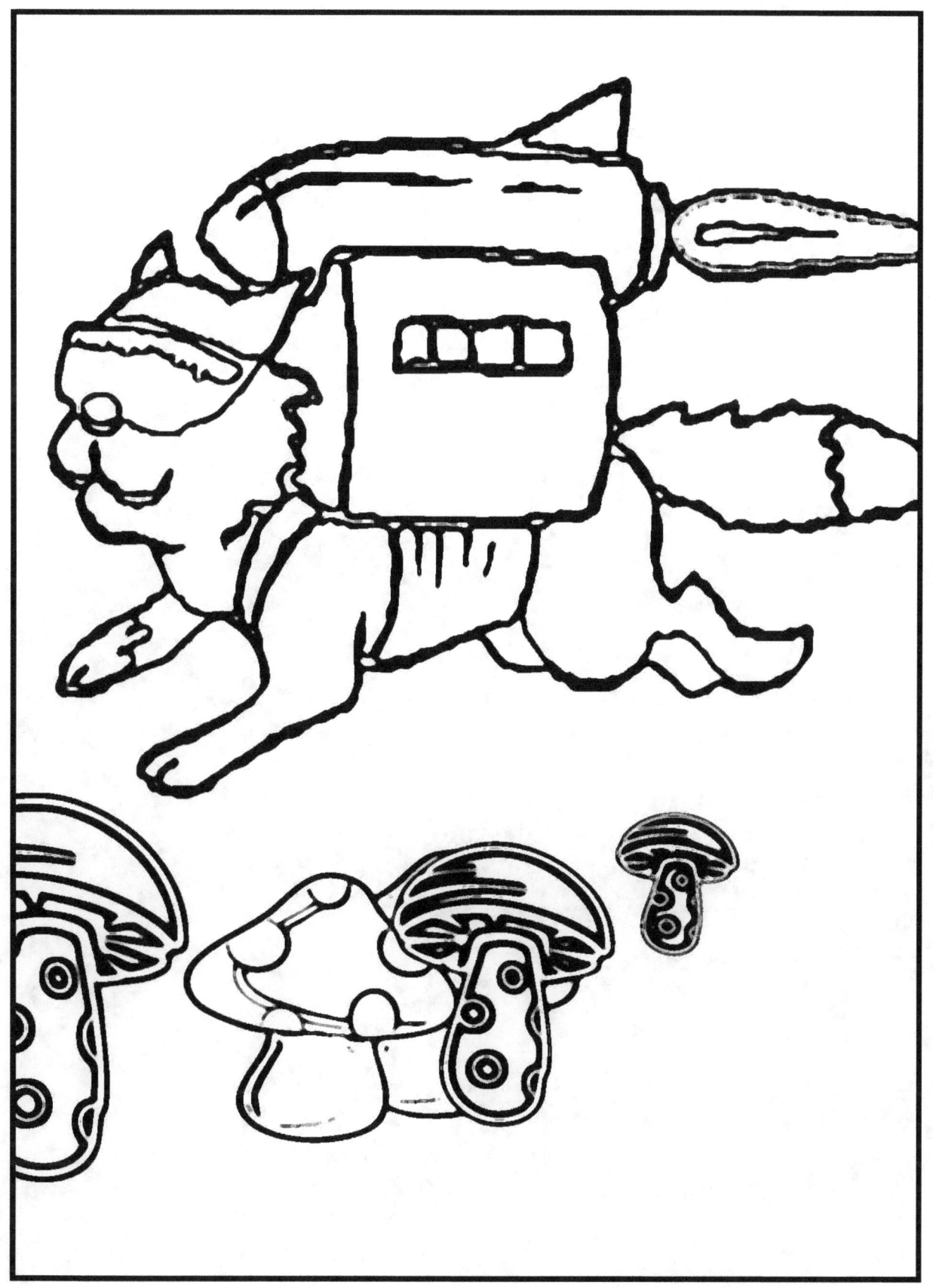

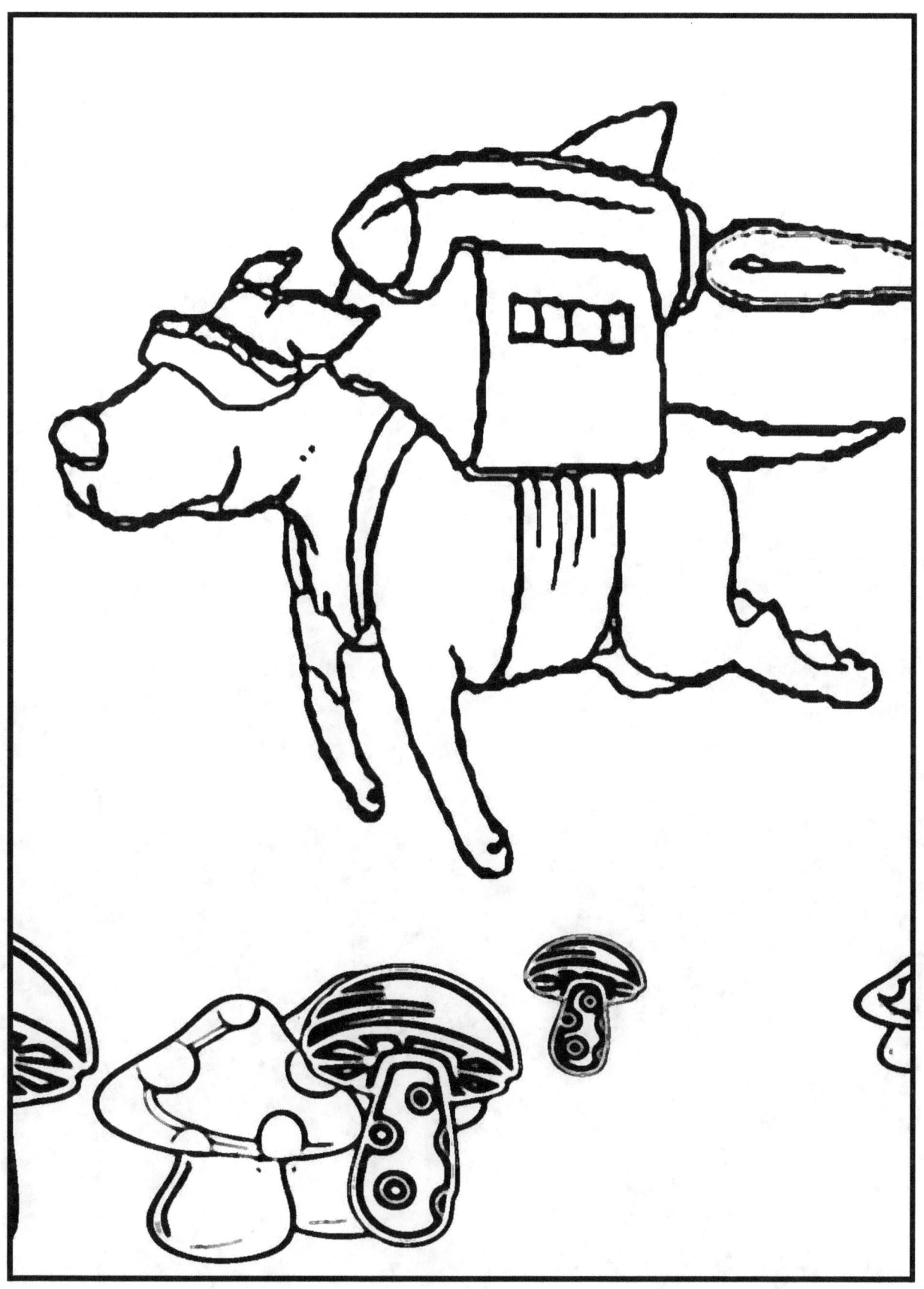

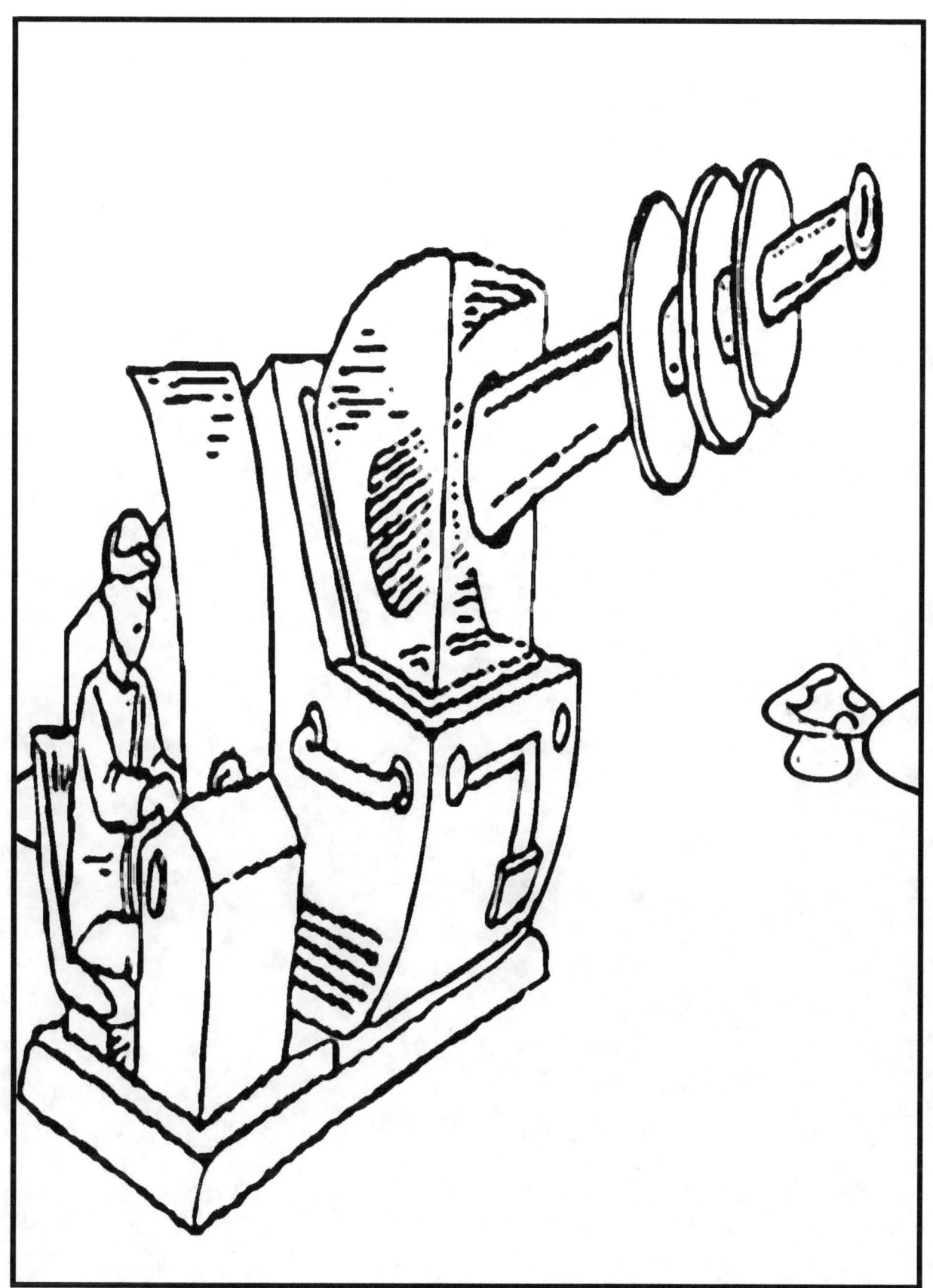

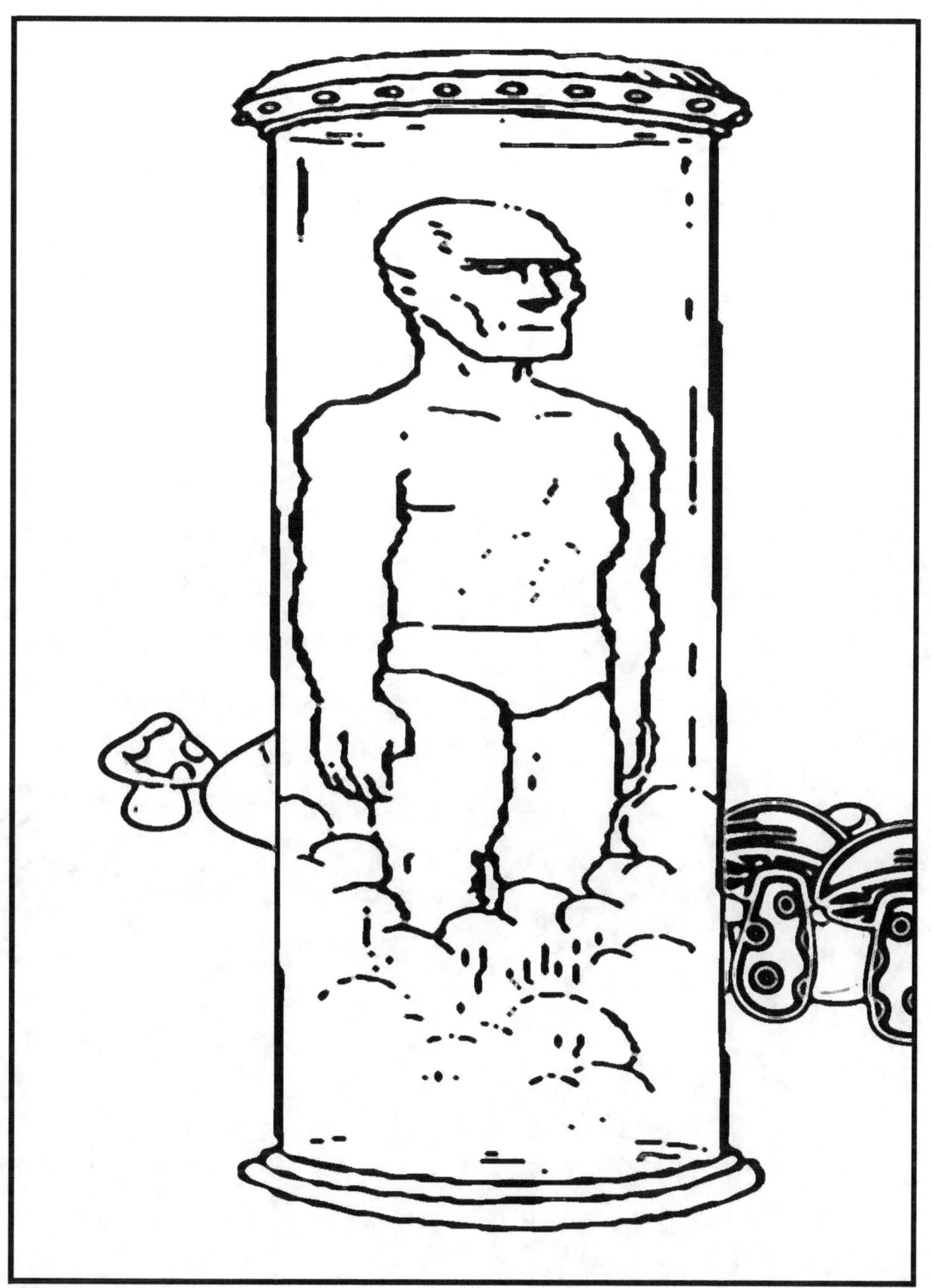

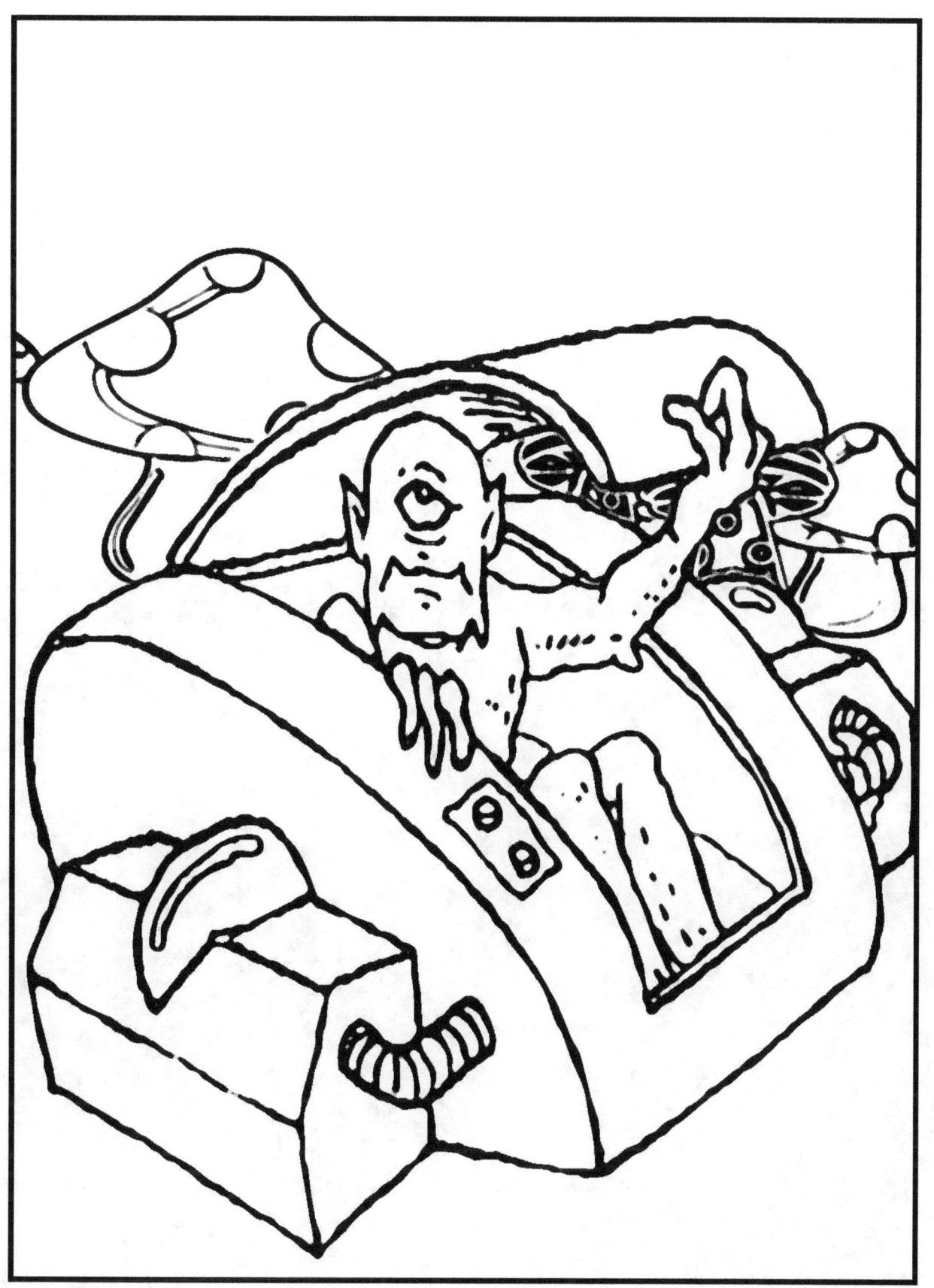

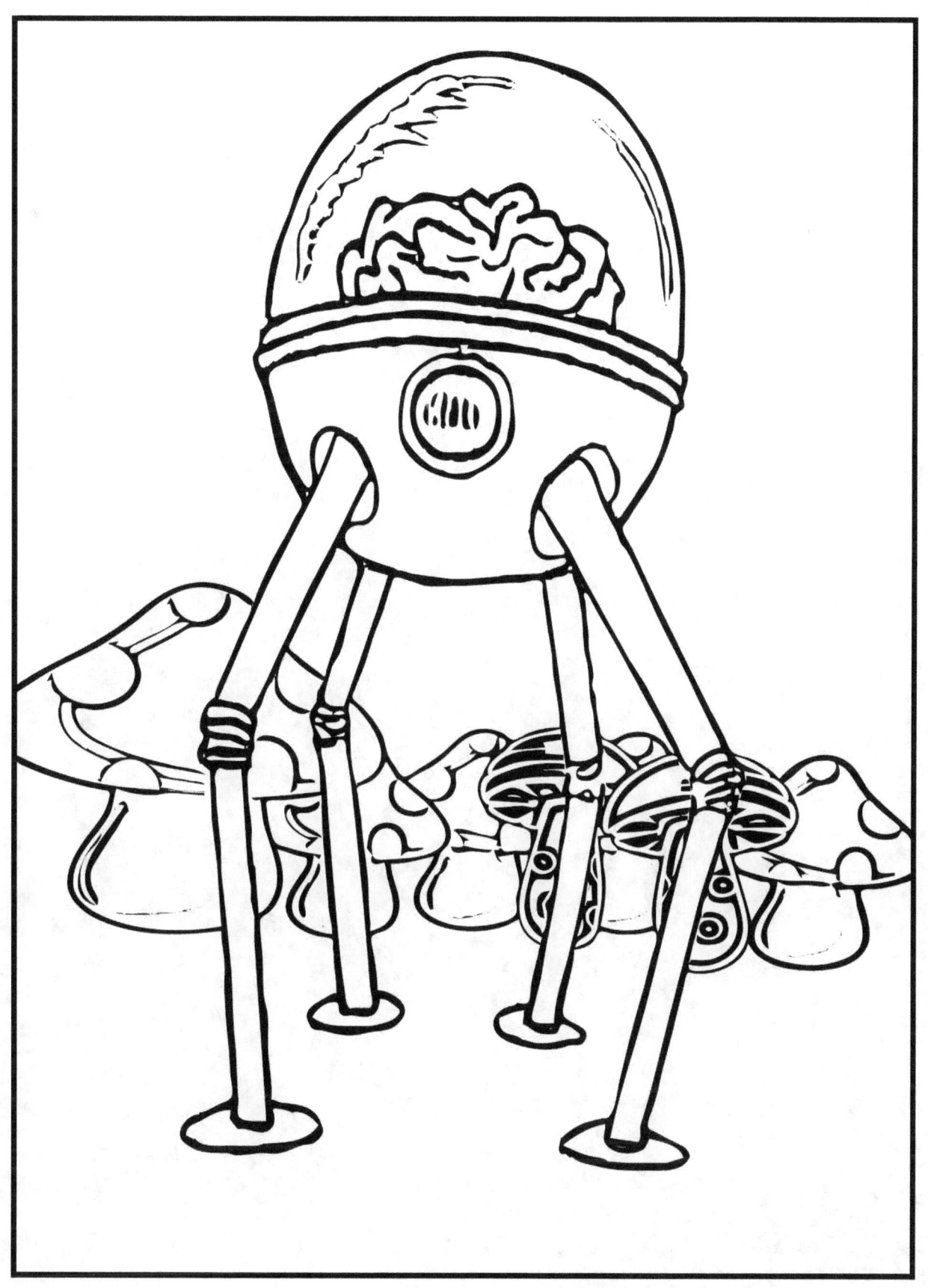

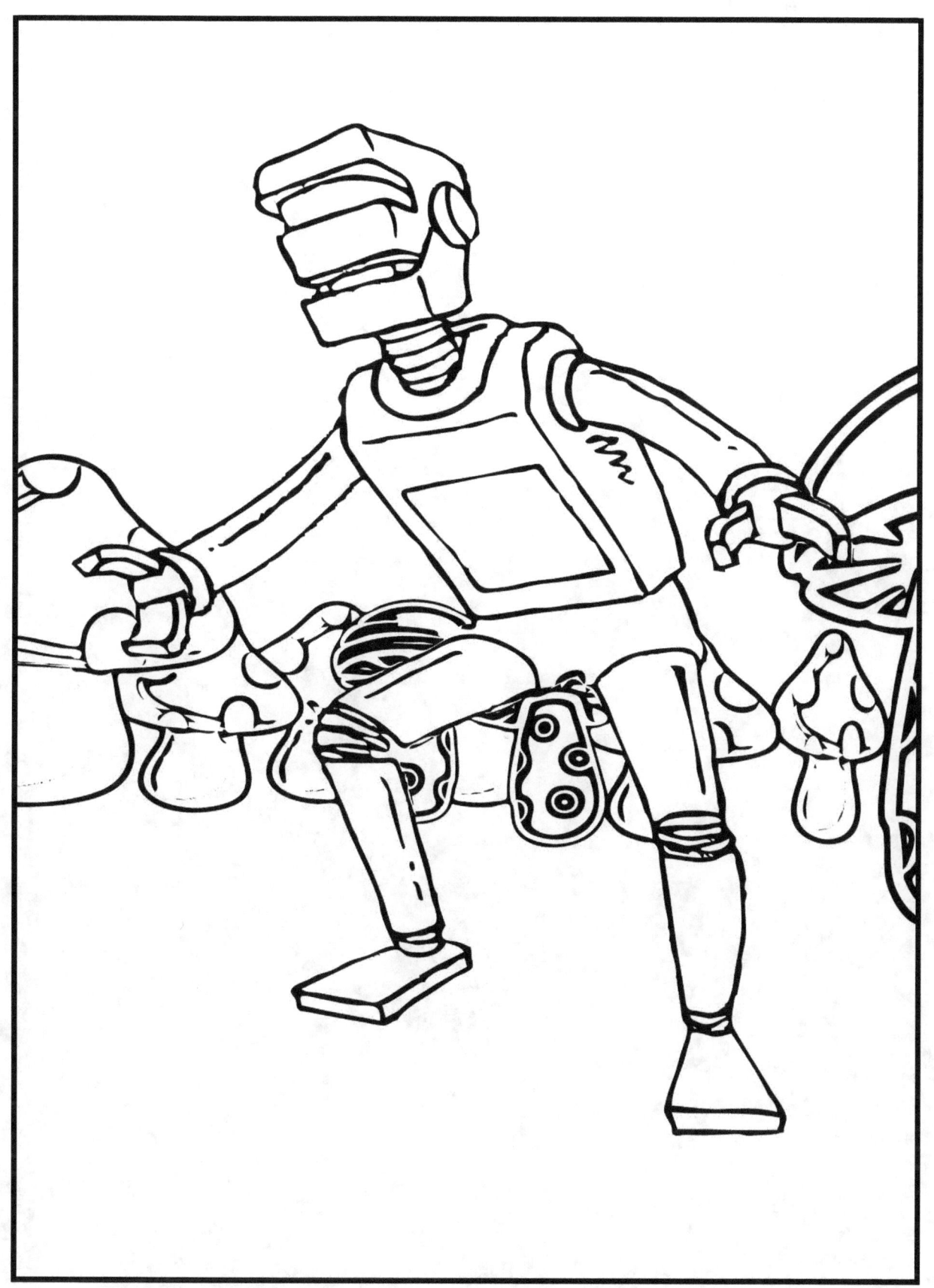

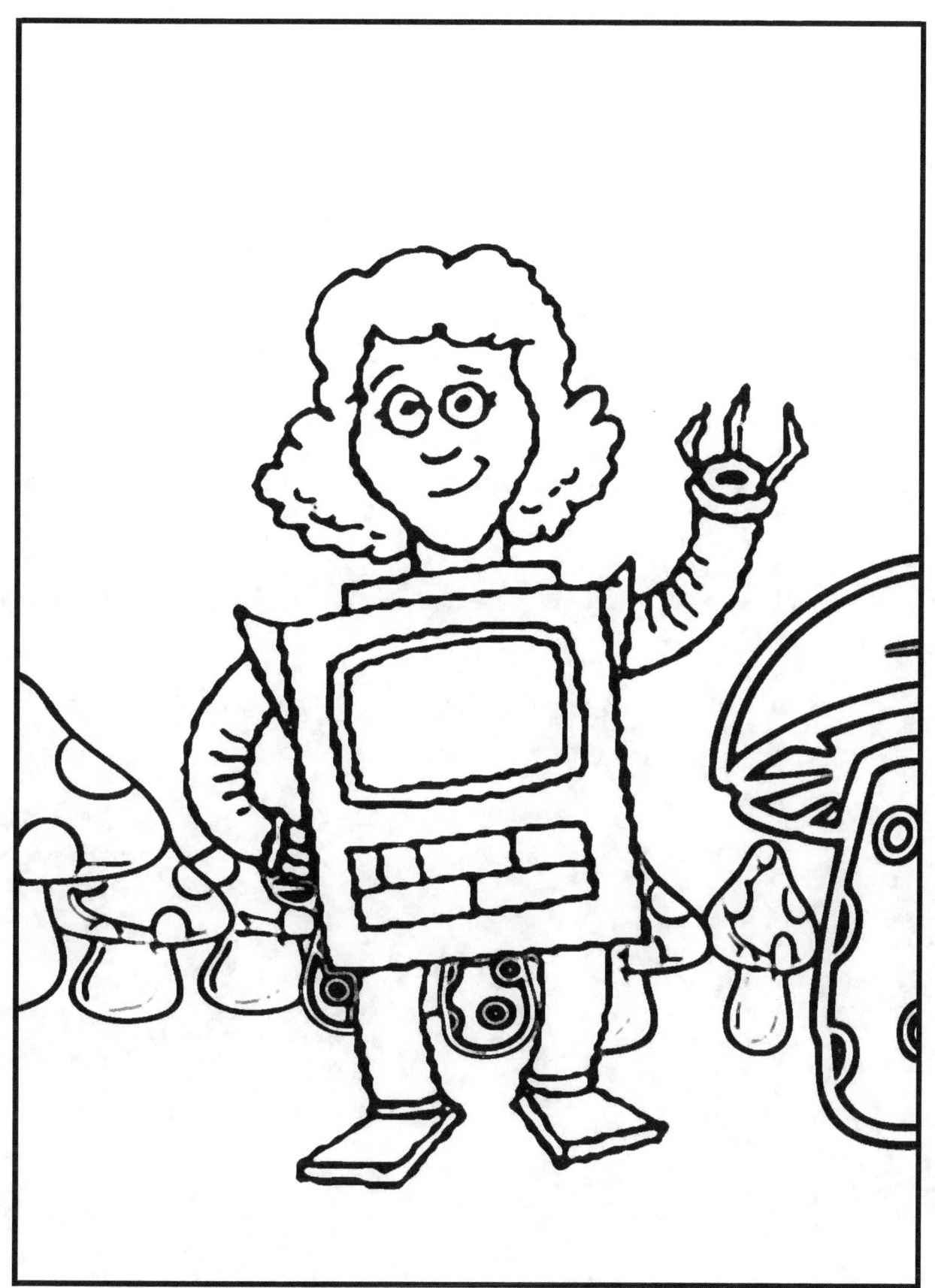

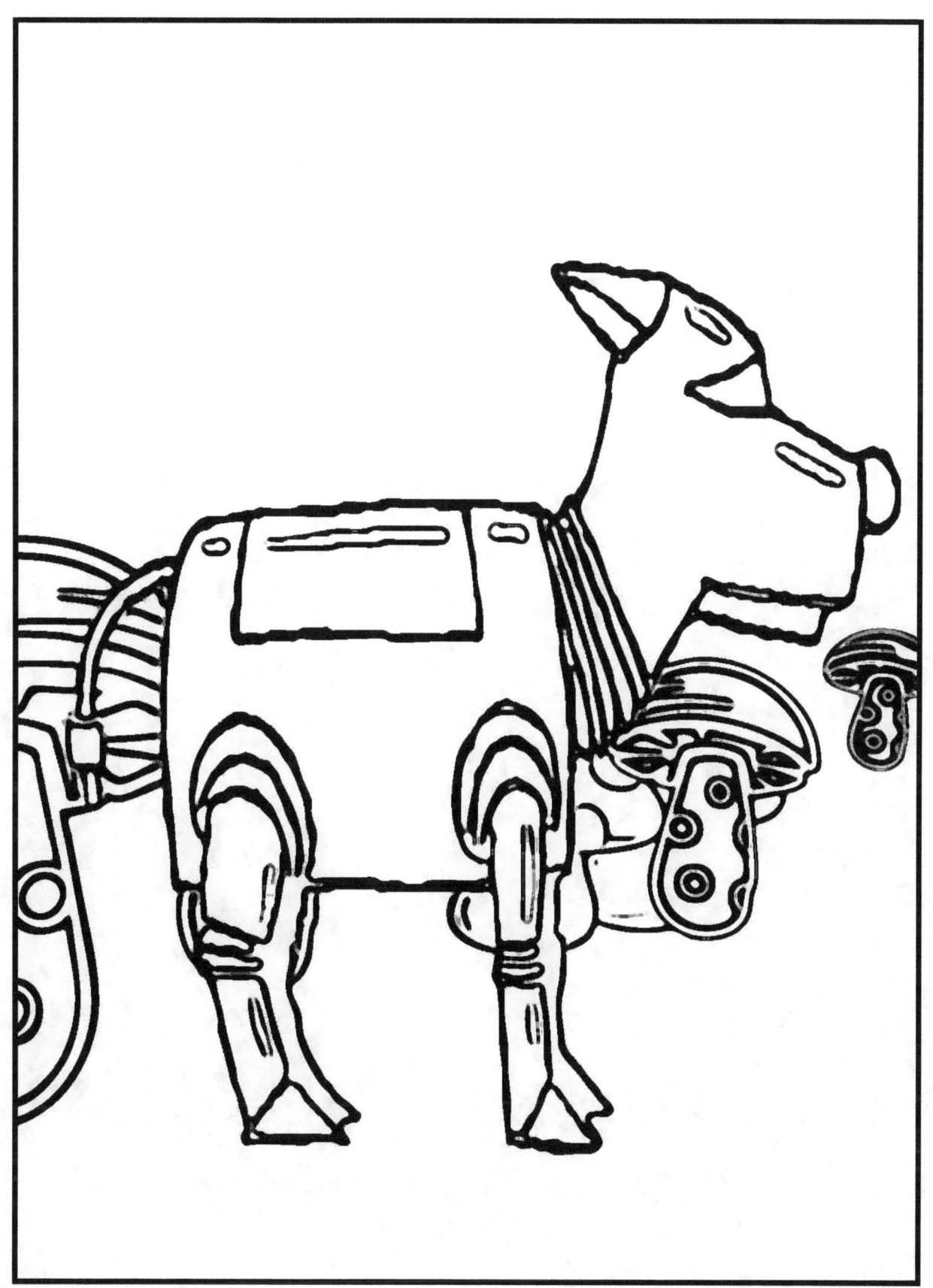

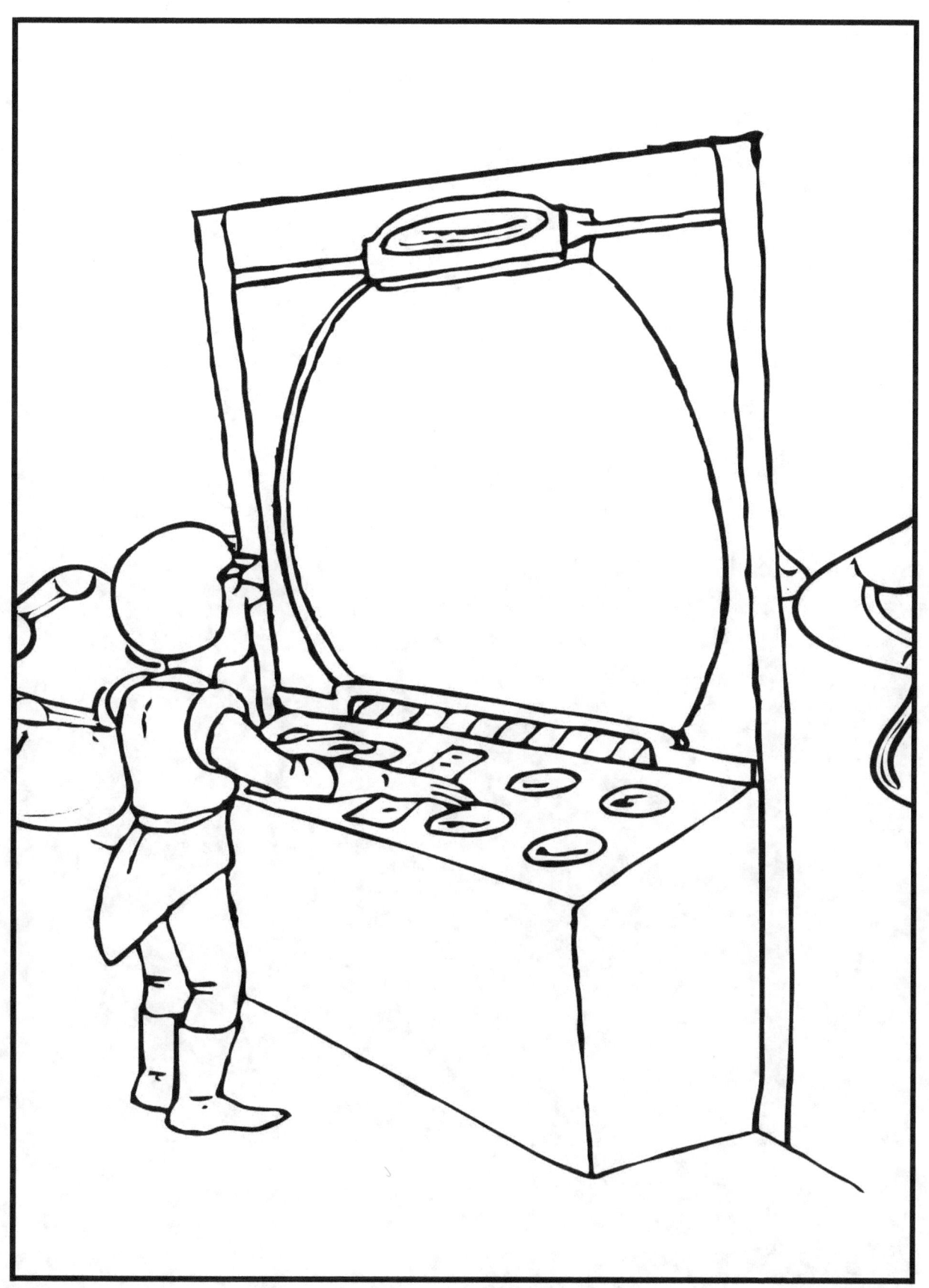

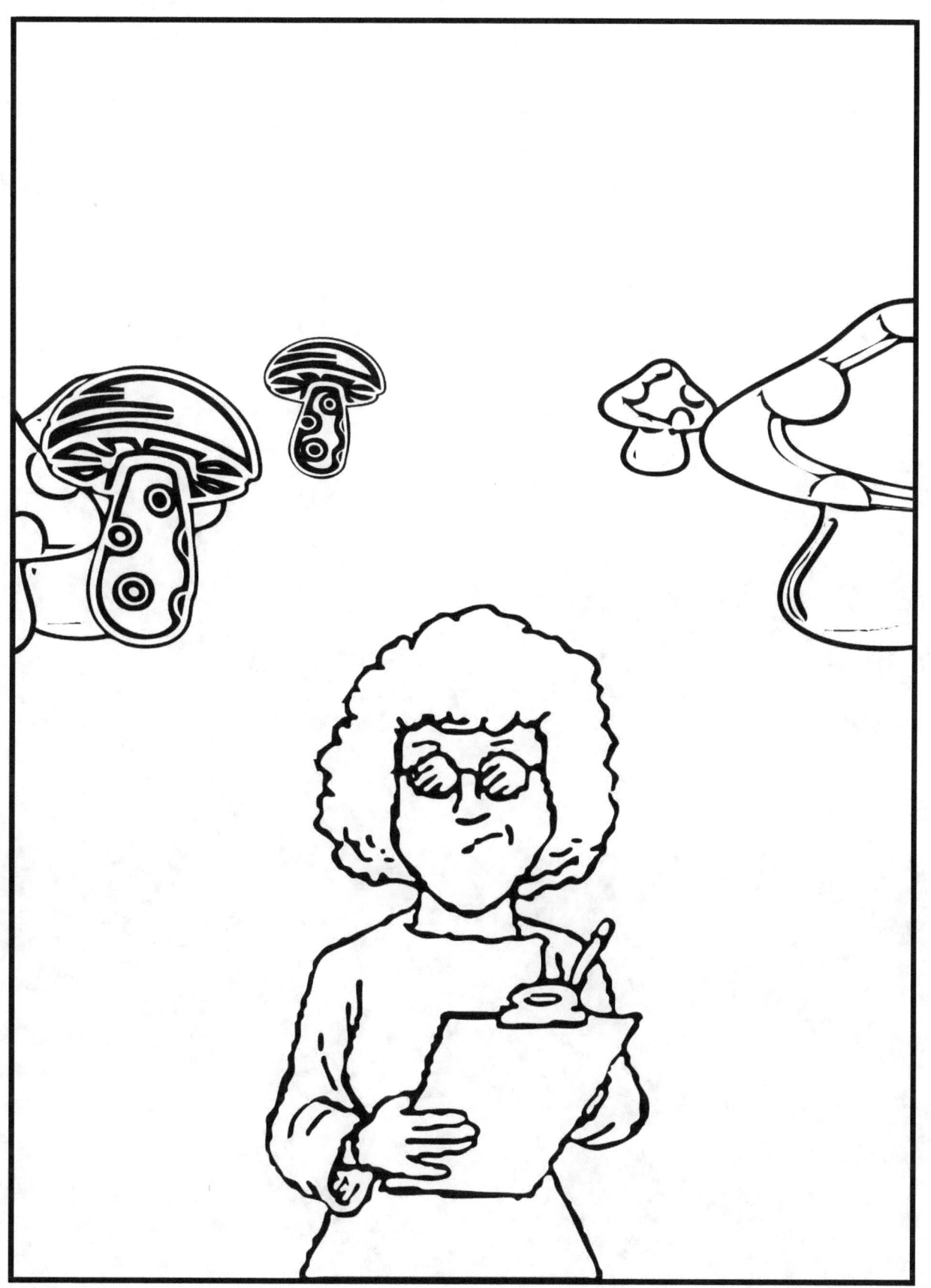

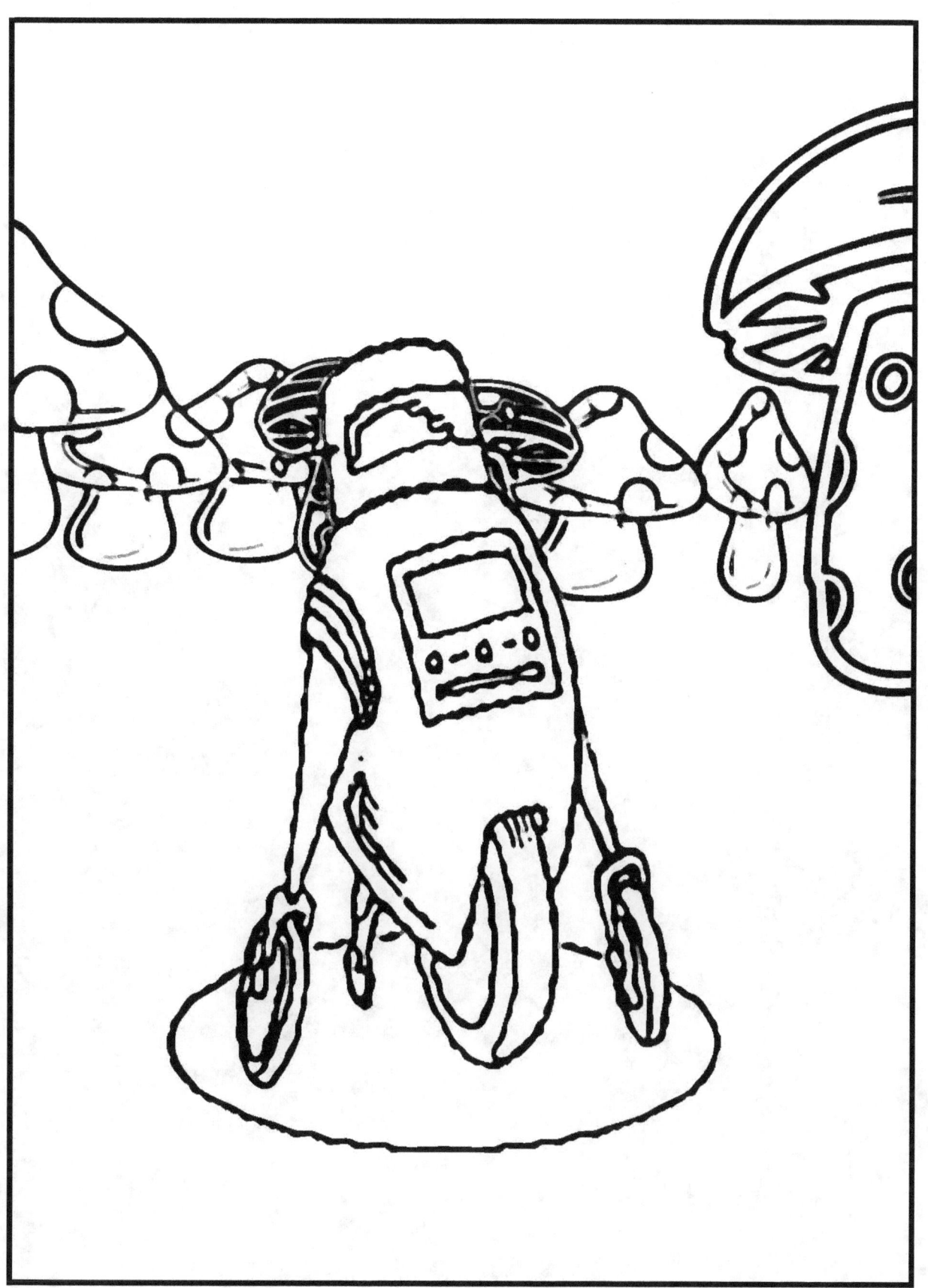

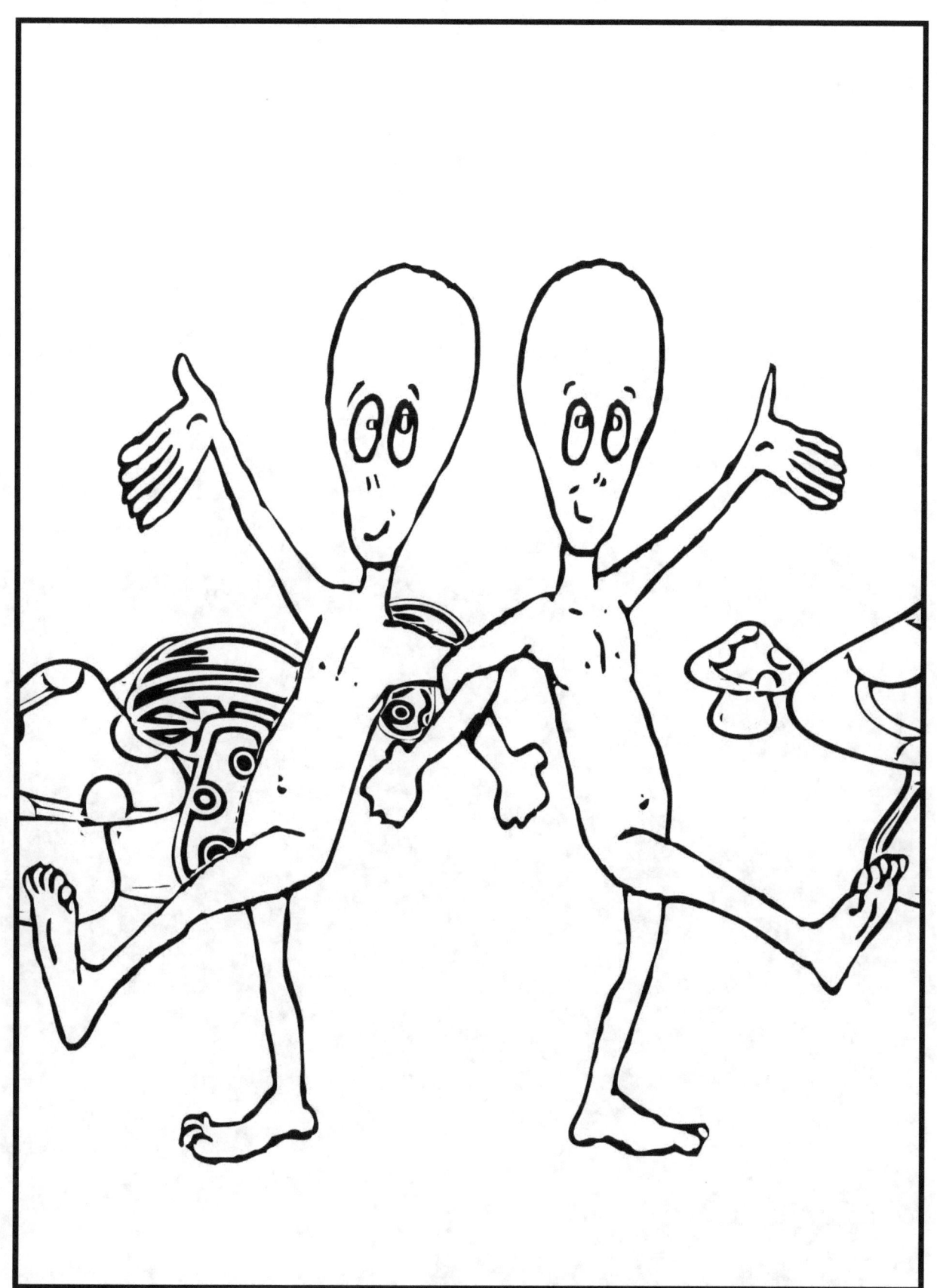

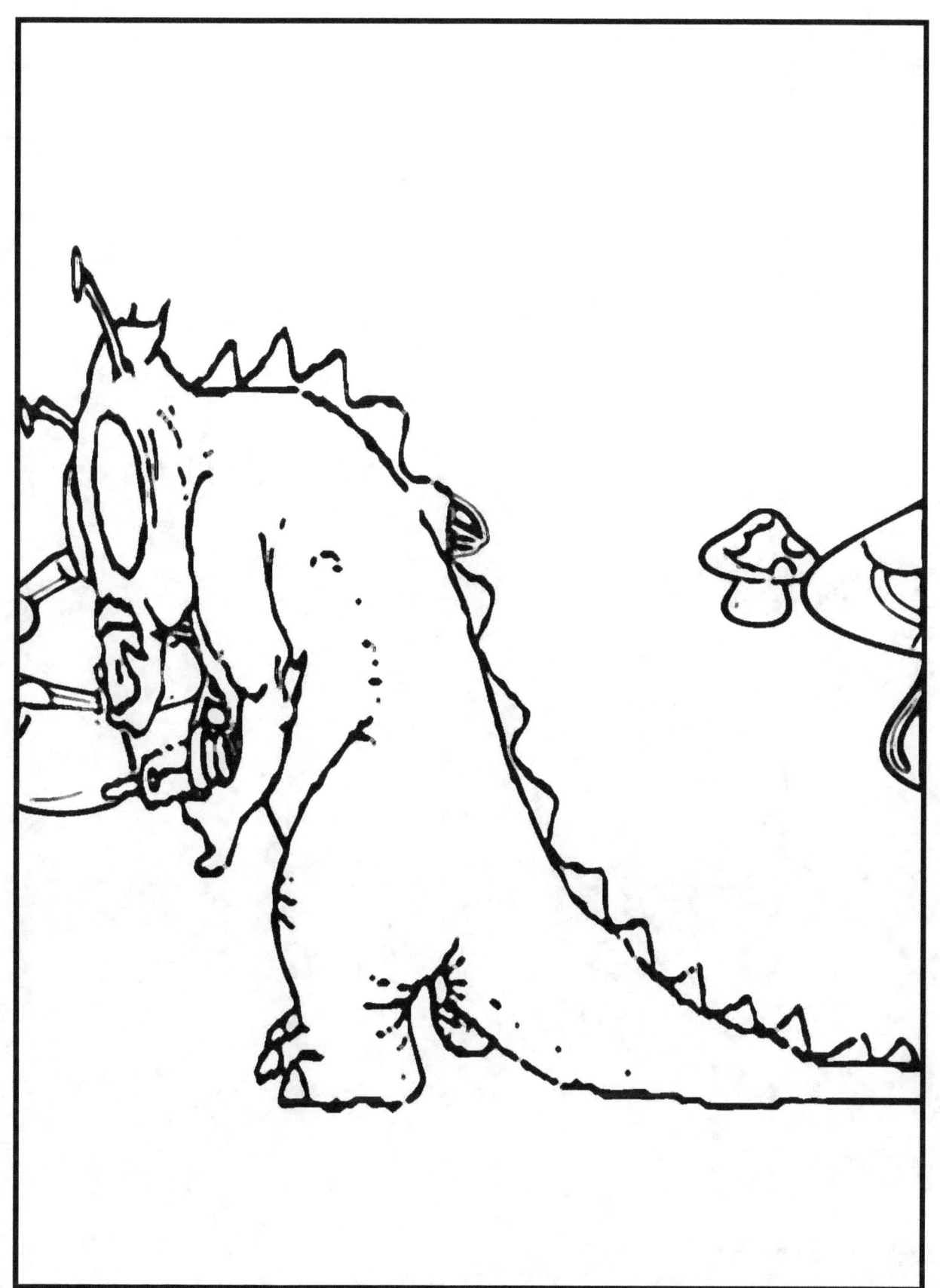

www.ingramcontent.com/pod-product-compliance
Lightning Source LLC
Chambersburg PA
CBHW081410170526
45166CB00010B/3288